FOCUS ON

FRANCE
AND THE FRENCH

ANITA GANERI

GLOUCESTER PRESS
New York · Chicago · London · Sydney

*First published in
the United States in 1993 by*
Gloucester Press
95 Madison Avenue
New York, NY 10016

Printed in Belgium

Design	David West Children's Book Design
Designer	Flick Killerby
Series Director	Bibby Whittaker
Editors	Jen Green, Suzanne Melia, Fiona Robertson
Picture research	Emma Krikler
Illustrators	David Burroughs Peter Kestevan David Russell Tessa Barwick

Library of Congress
Cataloging-in-Publication Data

Ganeri, Anita, 1961-
France and the French / Anita Ganeri.
p. cm — (Focus on)
Summary: Explores the geography, industries, climate, people, and culture of France.
Includes index.
ISBN 0-531-17401-8
1. France—Juvenile literature. [1. France.] I. Title. II. Series: Focus on (New York, N.Y.)
DC33.7.G34 1993
944—dc20 92-33479 CIP AC

INTRODUCTION

France is a beautiful country, rich in culture and steeped in history. Its capital, Paris, has for hundreds of years been renowned as a world center of art and learning, and many of the world's most famous writers and artists are French. France is a country of marked geographical contrasts, from the snow-capped Alps to the sunny beaches of the Mediterranean. It is also one of the world's leading agricultural and industrial nations.

This book offers an insight into France and the lives of the French people, bringing in related information from the fields of geography, language and literature, science and math, history, and the arts. The key below shows how the subjects are divided up.

Geography

The symbol of the planet Earth shows where geographical facts and activities are included. These sections include a look at the extent of French territory throughout the world.

Language and literature

An open book is the sign for activities that involve language and literature. In these sections, the influence of French literature is examined, and the works of such French writers as Hugo, Molière, and Rousseau are discussed.

Science and math

The microscope symbol indicates where a science project, math project, or science information is included. If the symbol is tinted green, it signals an environmental issue. A look at the perfume industry is included.

History

The sign of the scroll and hourglass shows where historical information is given. These sections look at key figures and events in French history and examine their contribution to society today.

Social history

The symbol of the family indicates where information about social history is given. Descriptions of festivals, holidays, rural and city life combine to create a flavor of France.

Art, crafts, and music

The symbol showing a sheet of music and art tools signals art, crafts, or musical activities. These sections look at French architecture and at the work of French artists.

CONTENTS

INFLUENCE AND PRESENCE

France is the largest country in western Europe and one of the most prosperous. It plays a key role in European and world affairs. The influence of French culture, food, and fashion has been felt all over the world. The map below shows where the French language is still spoken. Many of these countries were once part of the French Empire, but are now independent. France has a population of about 56 million. It covers an area of 213,000 square miles and includes the island of Corsica and several smaller islands in the Pacific Ocean and the Caribbean.

French departments and territories

1. Guadeloupe
2. Martinique
3. French Guiana
4. St. Pierre and Miquelon
5. Réunion
6. Mayotte
7. French Polynesia
8. Wallis and Fortuna
9. New Caledonia
10. Kerguelen Island
11. Crozet
12. Antarctic territories

North America

Europe

ATLANTIC

PACIFIC

South America

Africa

Antarctica

The *Tricolore*

The *Tricolore* (Tricolor) has been the national flag of the Republic of France since 1794. The red and blue represent the city of Paris, and the white is the traditional color of the French kings. Despite this link with royalty, these colors were adopted during the French Revolution as symbols of freedom (see pages 8/9). *La Marseillaise* has been the national anthem of France since 1795. It was composed by a soldier during the Revolution.

Great writers

France is famous for its writers, artists, and composers. Molière was the greatest French writer of comedy. Rousseau was a key figure in the eighteenth century.

Molière
1622-1673

Jean-Jacques Rousseau
1712-1778

The *fleur de lis* (see top left) and the cockerel (below) are famous symbols of France. The kings of France used the *fleur de lis* in heraldry. The cockerel represents the fighting spirit of the French.

French-speaking regions
13. Indochina
14. Algeria, Morocco, Tunisia, French Equatorial Africa, Cameroon
15. Belgium, Luxembourg, Switzerland
16. Québec

France in the EC
France is a leading member of the EC (European Community). This organization was set up to establish closer ties in trade, farming, law, and politics between the countries of Europe. The EC has grown out of the European Coal and Steel Community which France helped to found in 1951. It now has 12 member states (see map, page 31). The community can pass laws governing many aspects of life in the member countries. These include areas such as agriculture, the environment, health, food, education, transportation, and industry. A European Parliament, first elected in 1979, debates all policy issues.

Origins of language
French is a Romance language, derived from Latin. Until the 1500s, however, French was only spoken around Paris. Elsewhere, people spoke regional languages, such as Breton, and dialects. A standardized form of French, called *le bon usage*, was laid down in the 1530s by the writer Rabelais. Further Greek and Latin words were added during the Renaissance (1300-1600), resulting in a beautiful and harmonious language. In 1784, the French author Antoine Rivarol boasted "What is not clear, is not French."

French cuisine
French cooking and restaurants are renowned all over the world. The French consider cooking an art. They use only the best ingredients and like to linger over meals. Some of the most famous French delicacies are snails, crêpes, pâté, bouillabaisse (fish stew), and cassoulet (meat and bean casserole). They also consider wine an essential accompaniment to food and may drink more than one variety during a meal.

ORIGINS TO SUN KING

After the collapse of the Roman Empire in the fifth century A.D., France was conquered by a Germanic tribe called the Franks. France takes its name from the Franks. They ruled until A.D. 895, when Normandy in northern France was settled by Vikings from Scandinavia. They became known as the Normans. Later, it was the English who ruled over large areas of France. They were driven out in the sixteenth century, leaving the French kings to rule for the next 200 years.

Feudalism

In the Middle Ages (from the fifth to twelfth centuries), a system of labor called feudalism was in place in France. Aristocratic lords owned great estates of land. Peasants, called serfs, worked on the land and paid the lord rent in return for his protection. They had no land of their own and were known as tenants. They had no independence, but the protection of the lord was more important.

French prehistory

Prehistoric people lived in France as long ago as 15,000 B.C. Paintings dating from about that time were discovered in 1940 in caves in Lascaux, southwest France. Prehistoric artists had covered the walls with paintings of bulls, bisons, stags, horses, and lions. No one knows why people began to paint. Prehistoric people may have thought pictures had magical qualities.

Lascaux
wall painting

Charlemagne (top left) was the greatest and most powerful king of the Franks. He ruled from A.D. 771– 814. He was a great soldier, fighting over 50 military campaigns. Under his rule, the French Empire expanded to include parts of Spain, Germany, and northern Italy. Charlemagne was also a tireless campaigner on behalf of the pope and the Christian Church. In A.D. 800, he was crowned emperor of the Romans by Pope Leo III. After his death, the French Empire was split into three parts.

Joan of Arc

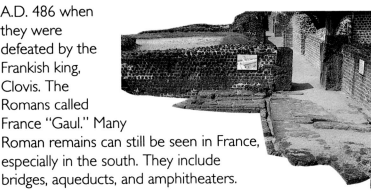

Louis XIV

Palace of Versailles

☐ Charlemagne's Empire in 771

▨ Area added after 771

The Romans in France
Roman armies began to invade France in about 200 B.C. Julius Caesar conquered France in 58–51 B.C. and the Romans ruled until A.D. 486 when they were defeated by the Frankish king, Clovis. The Romans called France "Gaul." Many Roman remains can still be seen in France, especially in the south. They include bridges, aqueducts, and amphitheaters.

Joan of Arc
Joan of Arc (Jeanne d'Arc) was born in 1412. As a young girl, she heard the voice of God telling her to fight the English and restore the French king to the throne. In 1429, Joan led the French army to victory at Orléans. In 1430, however, she was captured by the English and burned at the stake as a witch. Joan of Arc was made a saint in 1920.

Louis XIV - The Sun King
Louis XIV was nicknamed the "Sun King" because he was thought to be "the sun that lit up France." He ruled from 1643 to 1715, making France the most powerful country in Europe. Louis moved his court to Versailles, outside Paris, where he had a magnificent palace built (above).

REVOLUTION ONWARD

After Louis XIV died, France went into decline. Ordinary people were poor and hungry. They resented the huge sums of money spent on costly and unsuccessful wars. In 1789, they stormed the Bastille prison in Paris – the French Revolution had begun. The king, Louis XVI, was overthrown and members of the aristocracy were guillotined. France became a republic in 1792. Since this First Republic, France has passed through four other major periods of history (see page 9). Today's France is the Fifth Republic.

The storming of the Bastille, July 14, 1789

The Storming of the Bastille took place on July 14, 1789. An angry mob attacked and captured the prison. The revolutionaries introduced a charter of human rights, called *The Declaration of the Rights of Man* and the slogan, *Liberté, Egalité, Fraternité.* Bastille Day is still celebrated today in France as a national holiday.

Victor Hugo
The poet and writer Victor Hugo (1802-1885), was a monarchist who became a republican. For this, he was exiled by Napoléon III, but returned to Paris in 1870 where he was regarded as France's leading literary figure. Hugo's two best-known works are the novels *Les Misérables* and *The Hunchback of Notre Dame.*

Emperor Napoléon Bonaparte, who built the Arc de Triomphe, below

Napoléon Bonaparte
Napoléon Bonaparte (1769-1821) was a brilliant army general who seized power in 1799. In 1804, he had himself crowned emperor of France. Napoléon based his empire on that of the Romans, conquering most of Europe and beyond. In 1815, he was defeated by the British at the Battle of Waterloo. Napoléon abdicated and was exiled to the South Atlantic island of St. Helena, where he died in 1821.

World War I

France suffered very heavy losses in World War I (1914–1918). Over a million Frenchmen died and around 4 million were injured. The Germans invaded France soon after the war started. For over three years, the border between France and Belgium became the battle front. Some of the worst battles took place around the town of Verdun in northeast France.

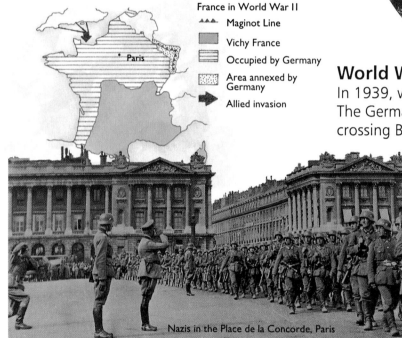

France in World War II

▲▲▲ Maginot Line

▦ Vichy France

▤ Occupied by Germany

▨ Area annexed by Germany

➧ Allied invasion

Paris

Troops in World War I

World War II

In 1939, war again broke out with Germany. The Germans invaded France in 1940, crossing Belgium to bypass the Maginot Line, a series of fortifications thought to be impassable. They occupied about two-thirds of France. Part of southern France remained under the control of the French Vichy Government. In 1942 the Germans took control of the area. France was liberated by the Allies in 1944.

Nazis in the Place de la Concorde, Paris

Toward a Fifth Republic

Today's France is called the Fifth Republic. This chart shows the dates of the other four.

1789............. The French Revolution
1792............. France becomes a republic
1804-1815 Reign of Napoléon I
1848............. The Second Republic
1852-1870 Reign of Napoléon III
1871............. The Third Republic
1914-1918 World War I
1939-1945 World War II
1946............. The Fourth Republic
1954-1962 War with Algeria
1958............. Charles De Gaulle establishes the Fifth Republic

De Gaulle

Crisis in Algeria

In the 1800s and early 1900s, the French Empire included many African and Asian colonies. By 1954, some had become independent, but the French refused to let Algeria go. War broke out in Algeria. In 1958, Charles De Gaulle (left), the leader of the Free French in World War II, was elected president, with special powers to tackle the crisis. He organized peace talks which led to a cease-fire in April 1962, and French voters approved Algeria's independence. Algeria became independent on July 3, 1962, and most French settlers there returned to France.

THE COUNTRY

The countryside of France ranges from fertile farmland around the river valleys to the snowcapped peaks of the Alps and Pyrénées. Mont Blanc, the highest mountain in Europe at 15,770 feet, is part of the French Alps. In the south lies the Côte d'Azur with its sandy beaches; in the center, the huge block of rugged mountains, called the Massif Central. The climate varies too. It is hotter in the south and west, which benefit from the warming effect of the Gulf Stream current. The Aquitanian lowlands in the southwest have pine forests, rolling plains, and sand dunes. Corsica lies 99 miles southeast of the mainland.

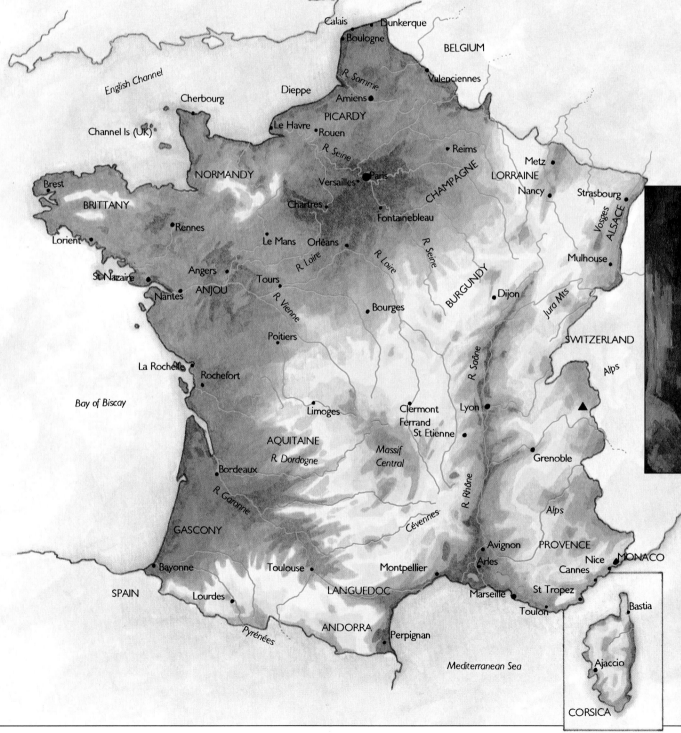

Calais
Dunkerque
Boulogne
BELGIUM
R. Somme
Valenciennes
English Channel
Dieppe
Amiens
Cherbourg
PICARDY
Le Havre
Rouen
Channel Is (UK)
R. Seine
Reims
Metz
LORRAINE
Brest
Versailles
Paris
CHAMPAGNE
Nancy
Strasbourg
NORMANDY
Chartres
Fontainebleau
Vosges
ALSACE
BRITTANY
Rennes
Le Mans
Orléans
R. Seine
Mulhouse
Lorient
R. Loire
R. Loire
Angers
Tours
BURGUNDY
Dijon
Jura Mts
St Nazaire
ANJOU
R. Vienne
Nantes
Bourges
SWITZERLAND
Poitiers
Alps
La Rochelle
Rochefort
R. Saône
Bay of Biscay
Limoges
Clermont Ferrand
Lyon
St Etienne
AQUITAINE
Massif Central
Grenoble
R. Dordogne
Bordeaux
R. Rhône
R. Garonne
Alps
Cévennes
GASCONY
Avignon
PROVENCE
Bayonne
Arles
Nice
MONACO
Toulouse
Montpellier
Cannes
SPAIN
Lourdes
LANGUEDOC
Marseille
St Tropez
Bastia
ANDORRA
Perpignan
Toulon
Pyrénées
Mediterranean Sea
Ajaccio
CORSICA

10

Separate identity

Many of the different groups of peoples in France want to preserve their own traditions and identity alongside their French nationality. The Bretons in the north-west have their own dress and language. In the south, the Provençal people also have their own language, which belongs to a group of dialects called Langue d'Oc. The Basques in the southwest and in Spain speak a language called Euskera. On Corsica, most of the population speak a dialect similar to Italian.

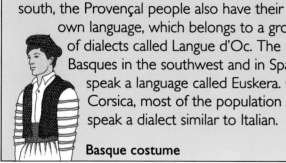

Breton dress is still worn by some older Bretons as part of everyday dress.

Savoy Alps costume

Basque costume

Images of landscape

The beauty of the French countryside inspired many of the French Impressionist painters. They tried to reproduce the immediate impression of a scene and the way light appears to the eye. Seurat and Cézanne were post-Impressionists. Cézanne painted Lac d'Annecy (left). He deliberately distorted the natural appearance of his subject to create a more dramatic composition. Seurat used a technique called pointillism (painting with individual dots of pure color)

in *The Bridge at Courbevoie* (above). Try this technique yourself. Look at your picture from a distance. Do the dots merge to form new colors?

The Camargue

The Camargue is a huge area of marshland in the south of France, where the River Rhône flows into the Mediterranean Sea. It was once famous for its huge herds of black bulls and white horses. The herds are smaller now, but the Camargue is still a vital habitat for hundreds of species of birds, including flamingos. The region is an important conservation area, where wildlife is protected.

CITIES AND TOWNS

Nearly three-quarters of French people live in cities and towns. Paris is by far the largest city (see pages 14/15). Other major cities include Marseilles, Lyon, Toulouse, and Nice. They are centers of trade, industry, and tourism. Most French cities are a mixture of old buildings and narrow streets, and modern apartments and offices. Many city centers are now traffic-free zones, with pleasant wide avenues (*boulevards*) and parks to stroll in. Sprawling suburbs have grown up around their outskirts. Public transportation systems carry people from the suburbs to a variety of jobs and recreational and cultural activities in the city.

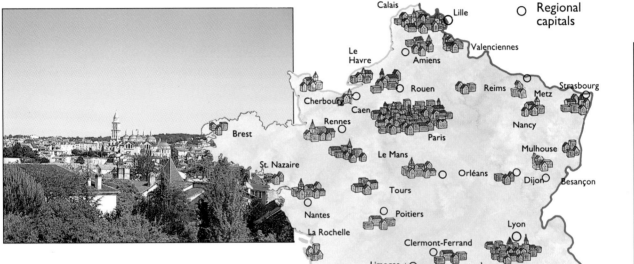

The largest cities of France are usually located near the coasts or along rivers. In comparison with Paris, other French cities are only medium-sized. They often contain historic buildings, most notably medieval cathedrals. Although most French people live in towns and cities, the increase in their populations has recently slowed down.

Working life

Many people live in the city suburbs and commute into the center each day to work. Over one-quarter of France's workforce is employed in manufacturing industries. They work in factories making cars, chemicals, aircraft, machinery, and so on. Many also work in service industries, for example, in restaurants and cafés, driving buses, or cleaning the streets. May 1 is officially celebrated as Workers' Day.

Although the monuments and old buildings of France's towns and cities are well preserved, there are also a lot of new apartment buildings, housing projects, and shopping centers. These tend to be located in the suburbs where there is more space and cheaper land. Strict regulations help to protect the center of many French cities and high-rise constructions may be limited by law.

City living

Sidewalk cafés are a major feature of life in French towns and cities. They are popular meeting places where people can eat, drink, and chat, or just watch the world go by. There are also museums, art galleries, and libraries to visit. Most cities and towns have open-air markets, selling fresh fruit and vegetables. The larger supermarkets, or hypermarkets, tend to be situated on the outskirts of the city.

Traditional architecture

France has much fine, traditional architecture, dating from the Middle Ages (500s to 1500s) to the present day. Gothic cathedrals dominated French architecture from about 1150 to 1300. Chartres cathedral (center) is a masterpiece of Gothic architecture. Gothic architects developed flying buttresses, which were brick or stone supports built against the outside walls. Ribbed vaults in the ceilings were also a distinctive characteristic.

Flying buttress

A more recent French architect, Le Corbusier (1887–1965), led a movement known as the International Style. The major elements of his designs are a geometric shape, white concrete walls, a flat roof, and a continuous band of windows.

Rib vault ceiling

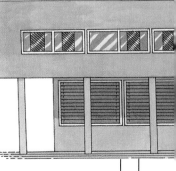

Building by Le Corbusier

PARIS

Paris is France's largest city and its capital. It is the political, industrial, and cultural center of France. It is also one of the most picturesque and most visited cities in the world. Paris's world-famous sights include the Eiffel Tower, Montmartre, and the Champs-Elysées with its many art galleries and fashion boutiques. There are also many fine hotels, restaurants, and theaters. The cathedral of Notre Dame stands on the Ile de la Cité. This is the oldest part of Paris. It is the area where the city was founded about 2,000 years ago by the Romans.

An island in the River Seine, the Ile de la Cité, is the heart of Paris. As the city grew, it soon spread out on both banks of the river. The original city wall has long since disappeared, replaced by the broad, tree-lined *boulevards* built between 1853 and 1870. The River Seine curves through Paris for about 8 miles from east to west, enclosed by high stone embankments and crossed by many bridges.

Key
1. Palais de Chaillot
2. Eiffel Tower
3. Arc de Triomphe
4. Les Invalides
5. Place de la Concorde
6. Opéra de la Bastille
7. Sacré-Coeur
8. La Bourse (Stock Exchange)
9. Le Louvre
10. Centre Georges-Pompidou
11. Notre Dame
12. Panthéon
13. Palais du Luxembourg

Modern architecture

In 1989, a modern glass pyramid was built over the entrance to the Louvre, causing huge controversy. One of the biggest and most famous art galleries in the world, the Louvre houses the *Mona Lisa* by Leonardo da Vinci. The sculptured iron entrances to the Métro were also a new style to Parisians in 1900. They are a fine example of Art Nouveau.

Pyramid of
the Louvre

Métro entrance

METROPOLITAIN

Paris fashion

Paris is one of the main centers of the fashion world. It has been a fashion center since the fourteenth century, but the modern fashion industry began in the nineteenth century. Each spring, designers from all over the world come to view the work of fashion houses such as Yves St. Laurent, Chanel, and Christian Dior. The Paris collections influence fashion and are copied all over the world.

Art in Montmartre

The white church of the Sacré-Coeur (Sacred Heart) stands on a hill overlooking the district of Montmartre. This was once the haunt of famous artists, such as Toulouse-Lautrec, Renoir, and Picasso. The district's music halls, cafés, and bars inspired many of Toulouse-Lautrec's paintings. He was also famous for his posters, advertising nightclubs and various other products.

La Défense (below) was opened in 1978. It is a huge complex containing offices, shops, entertainment, and sports facilities. Modern sculptures, trees, and fountains decorate the complex's pedestrian precinct.

The modern Centre Pompidou (above) was opened in 1977. It contains the National Museum of Modern Art. All its pipes, vents, and ducts are on the outside, painted in greens, reds, and blues.

Right and left banks

The River Seine flows through Paris, dividing the city into the Left Bank and Right Bank. Traditionally, the Right Bank has been the business center of the city. The Left Bank is where intellectuals, such as the writer and philosopher Jean-Paul Sartre, lived and worked. The Sorbonne (Paris's university) and the student Latin Quarter are on the Left Bank. This area has been called the Latin Quarter since the Middle Ages, when teachers and students spoke in Latin.

Jean-Paul Sartre
1905–1980

RURAL FRANCE

Only about one-quarter of French people live in the countryside. The rest live in towns and cities (see pages 12/13). As a result, the French countryside is relatively spacious and uncrowded. It is dotted with farms and villages. Most country people make their living by farming (see pages 22/23). Villages are often very old. The center point of a village is usually a small square surrounded by a church, the Mairie (town hall), shops, and cafés. This is where people meet to chat or to play *boule* (see pages 20/21).

Once or twice a week, the village has its market day. Markets are often held in the village square. Local farmers come to sell their vegetables, fruit, dairy products, and poultry. There may also be stalls selling clothes, household goods, and flowers. The market is a traditional part of French rural life. It is not only a place for shopping, but also for meeting with friends. Villages and small towns also rely on local shops. Many specialize in one kind of product, like cheese.

Festivals

Many French festivals and holidays are connected to the Church, such as saints' days, Christmas, and Easter. There are also smaller village festivals celebrating local produce. These include wine, lavender, and cheese festivals, oyster festivals, and even nougat festivals. The sign below advertises a festival to celebrate the local agricultural product, in this case pigs. Most villages honor their local patron saints with a festival in July.

Lace making

Traditional lace is made by braiding, twisting, and knotting strands of linen or silk together, by hand. The town of Alençon in Normandy has been a lace-making center for over 300 years, and still has a lace-making school. Try knotting cord yourself, as below. Tie four loops of different colors over the pins, and follow the diagram. Start by knotting threads A and D together, over B and C. Then H and C, over D and G, and so on.

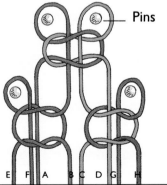

Pins

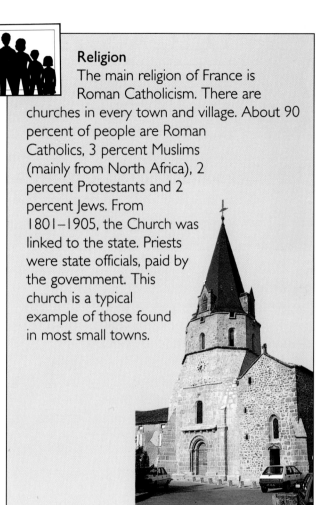

Religion

The main religion of France is Roman Catholicism. There are churches in every town and village. About 90 percent of people are Roman Catholics, 3 percent Muslims (mainly from North Africa), 2 percent Protestants and 2 percent Jews. From 1801–1905, the Church was linked to the state. Priests were state officials, paid by the government. This church is a typical example of those found in most small towns.

Market day is a busy and exciting day in most French towns. The streets and cafés are crowded.

The *châteaux*

There are *châteaux* all over France. Some are small manor houses; others are magnificent palaces that once belonged to kings and the aristocracy. The most famous *châteaux* are those in the Loire Valley. Many date from the Renaissance period in the sixteenth century. The best examples include those at Fontainebleau, Chambord, and Azay-le-Rideau. Many *châteaux* have their own vineyards and are famous for their wine production.

Château de Lavauguyon (below) is situated in the district of Haute-Vienne. It is a fine example of impressive Renaissance architecture.

The Château Prieuré-Lichine (left) is a small wine-producing manor house in the Médoc region.

ORGANIZATION

France is a republic (*La République Française*) with a democratically elected government. The president is head of state and is elected for seven years at a time. The president can serve an unlimited number of terms and appoints the prime minister. The prime minister, or premier, is head of the government and chooses who will serve on the cabinet (the Council of Ministers). Parliament is made up of two houses. The National Assembly has over 500 members, called deputies. The Senate has over 300 members, called Senators.

The offices and official residences of the president, prime minister, and the various government bodies are all in Paris. They are located in many historic and impressive buildings, as follows:

President - Palais de l'Elysée
Prime Minister - Hôtel Matignon
Seat of Parliament - Chambre des Deputés
National Assembly - Palais Bourbon
Senate - Palais du Luxembourg
Supreme Administrative Court - Palais Royal

Currency

The *franc* (F or f) is the unit of currency used in France. It is divided into 100 smaller units, called *centimes* (c). Some people still do their calculations in old francs, which were in use until 1959. There were 100 old francs to one new franc. A French franc has the words "République Française" on one side and the motto "Liberté, Egalité, Fraternité" on the other.

The president of France lives in the Palais de l'Elysée (top), built in 1718. The main house of parliament, the National Assembly, meets in the Palais Bourbon (above), completed in 1728. The National Assembly is more powerful than the Senate and makes the final decisions.

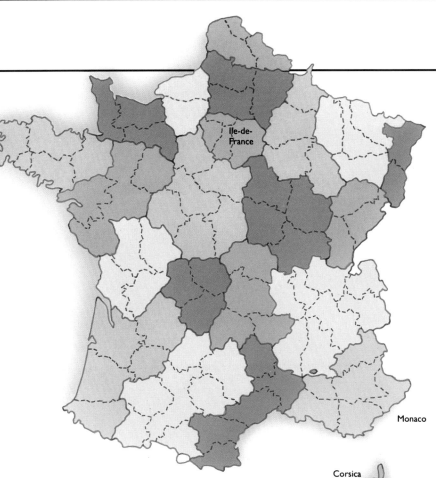

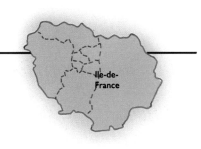

Ile-de-France

Monaco

Corsica

Départements

France is divided into 22 local government regions. These are further divided into 96 areas, called *départements*. Each *département* has its own number which is used as a postal code and on car registration plates. Each *département* has a commissioner who reports to the national government in Paris. Each of the 22 regions has a regional council, elected by the people, and a president elected by the council members. The Paris region is divided into eight *départements*, known as the *Ile-de-France.* The smallest unit of local government is the *commune,* which ranges in size from villages to cities.

The Palais du Luxembourg (above) is the meeting place of the Senate. The palace was built during the early 1600s. The Palais Royal (right) is the meeting place of the Supreme Administrative Court.

The legal system

The French legal system is based on the system used by the Romans. The highest court in the land is the Court of Cassation. It can hear appeals from the regional criminal and civil courts, and has the power to review cases and overturn decisions. The Court of Assizes hears cases of murder and other serious crimes. French judges are appointed by the minister of justice. They hold their positions for life. The French police force is known as *La Police* and the policemen are called *les agents de police.* *Gendarmes* (top left) belong to a branch of the French military.

19

EDUCATION AND LEISURE

Education is very important in France, but so are sports and leisure. Sports, such as football, cycling, tennis, horse racing, and rugby, are followed very closely. French people have about five weeks vacation each year. Many head to the mountains for skiing, or to the coasts where they like to sail, swim, and windsurf. They also enjoy going to cafés and restaurants, and to the movies and theater.

The annual *Tour de France* is one of the most important sporting events in France. Over one hundred top class cyclists take part in the race, which lasts for 26 days. The cyclists cover about 2,975 miles of France. The race finishes in Paris.

From the ages of two to six, many children go to nursery schools. From six to eleven, they attend primary school. They go to a *collège* from the age of eleven to fifteen. Then they go to a general *lycée* to study for the *baccalauréat* examination, or to a vocational *lycée* to train for a job. If students pass the *"bac,"* they can go to college. There are 75 universities in France, together with the more élite grandes écoles.

Boule

Boule, or *pétanque*, is the national game of France. It can be played in any flat, open space, such as a village square or a park track. It is a similar game to bowls, or lawn bowling. The winner is the player whose boule is closest to the jack.

1. The first player (red) draws a circle to stand in and throws the *cochonnet* (jack) 20-30 feet forward.

2. Then he throws his first boule as close to the jack as possible. He must remain inside the circle as he throws.

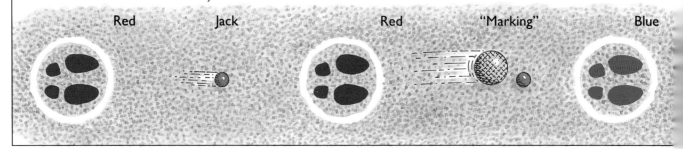

Red   Jack   Red   "Marking"   Blue

Gérard Depardieu

The theater and films are very popular with French people. Famous names of French films include Brigitte Bardot and Gérard Depardieu. Each year, in April and May, the International Film Festival is held in Cannes in southeastern France. Actors, actresses, and filmmakers from all over the world go there to promote their latest films. The *Comédie Française* in Paris is the most famous theater in France. It was established in 1680 by King Louis XIV. It is the state theater of France and all the best plays are performed there.

Braille

Braille is a system of writing and printing for blind people. It was invented by Louis Braille (1809–1852). He had been blinded in an accident at the age of three. The braille system uses six raised points, used in over 60 combinations. Blind people read braille by running their fingers along the dots.

Louis Braille

All for one ...

French authors are world famous not only for their adult work but for their children's writing too. Alexandre Dumas (1802-1870) wrote his best-known novel, *The Three Musketeers*, in 1844. Jules Verne wrote *Around the World in Eighty Days* (1873), and Charles Perrault (1628-1703) is best known for a book of fairy tales. Published in 1697, *Tales of Mother Goose* included "Sleeping Beauty," "Puss in Boots," and "Cinderella."

3. The second player (blue) stands in the circle and tries to throw her boule closer to the jack.

4. The person farthest away (red) can try to knock the other boule out of play or get nearer to the jack himself.

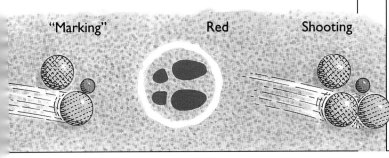

"Marking"   Red   Shooting

Astérix is a popular character among children and adults. The adventures of *Astérix the Gaul*, by Goscinny and Uderzo, have been translated into every major language.

AGRICULTURE AND FOOD

Agriculture is very important in France. Over half of the land is used for farming. Food and farm goods make up about one-fifth of France's exports. Farmers raise animals such as beef and dairy cattle, sheep, poultry, and pigs. Fish and seafood are caught along the west coast and the Mediterranean. Among the main crops grown are sugar beet, wheat and other cereal crops, and fruit, such as grapes and apples. France produces about one-quarter of the world's wine – only Italy produces more. France also produces some 400 varieties of cheese, many of which are world famous.

Many regions and towns in France are known throughout the world for their wine, cheese, mustard, and so on. The map below shows just a small selection of famous French foods.

Huge fields of sunflowers light up the countryside of southern France. Their seeds are harvested and used to make sunflower oil for cooking and margarine. A sunflower head may measure more than 20 inches across.

Most of France's wheat crop is grown around Paris and in the north. This is where the biggest, and richest, farms are to be found.

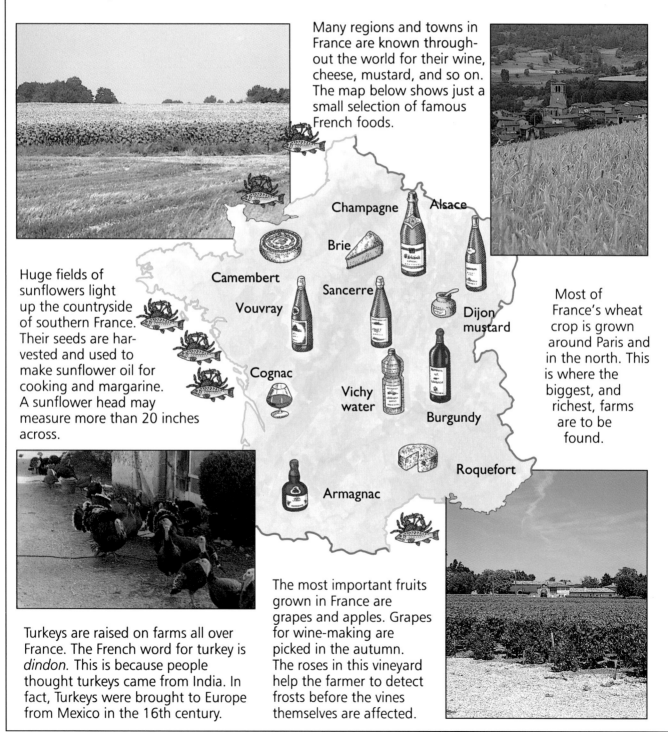

Champagne
Alsace
Brie
Camembert
Vouvray
Sancerre
Dijon mustard
Cognac
Vichy water
Burgundy
Roquefort
Armagnac

Turkeys are raised on farms all over France. The French word for turkey is *dindon.* This is because people thought turkeys came from India. In fact, Turkeys were brought to Europe from Mexico in the 16th century.

The most important fruits grown in France are grapes and apples. Grapes for wine-making are picked in the autumn. The roses in this vineyard help the farmer to detect frosts before the vines themselves are affected.

Wine-making

To make white wine, white and red grapes are crushed (1), then pumped into a press (2). The juice goes into a vat to ferment (3). It is fermented completely to make dry wine (6), half fermented for sweet wine (4), or bottled early to make sparkling wine (5). The dry wine may be distilled (7) to make brandy (8). To make red wine, red grapes are crushed (9) and fermented in a vat, usually with their skins (12). Some wine is drawn off after about two weeks (13). It is then pressed and squeezed (15) with the skins (14). Rosé (17) is made in the same way, but drawn from the vat (12) earlier and put in a second vat to ferment (16). Fortified wines (18) are made from trodden red grapes (10). The juice is fermented (11), then mixed with brandy from the still (7).

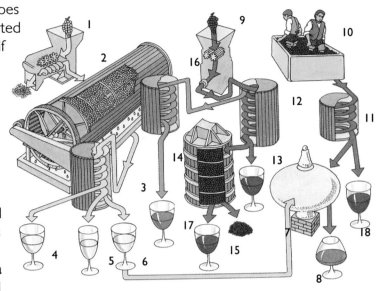

Louis Pasteur

Louis Pasteur (1822–1895) was a chemist and biologist. He found that diseases are spread by bacteria (germs). Pasteur also found that bacteria could turn milk and beer sour. He developed a process, now known as pasteurization, which uses heat to kill the bacteria. It is still used today to make milk safe. Pasteur became director of the Pasteur Institute in Paris (see page 29).

A la carte

A French restaurant is an ideal place to learn about French food and practice your French. Here are some words to help you with the menu:

la carte - menu
le couvert - place setting
les hors d'oeuvres - starters
le potage - soup
le poisson - fish
la viande - meat
les pommes frites - fries
le pain - bread

le beurre - butter
les légumes - vegetables
le fromage - cheese
la glace - ice cream
la crêpe - pancake
le café au lait - coffee with milk
le vin rouge - red wine
le vin blanc - white wine

Bon appétit! Enjoy your meal!

Making a crêpe

To make a thin French pancake, or crêpe, sift two ounces of plain flour and a pinch of salt into a bowl. Add an egg, 3 tablespoons of milk, and one of oil. Mix the batter well. Leave it for an hour, then pour a little into a hot frying pan.

INDUSTRY AND EXPORT

France is one of the world's leading industrial countries. A program of modernization began in the 1950s. As a result, France now has important iron and steel, car, and chemical industries. It is in the top five of world exporters and sells its goods to almost every country. France is at the forefront of technology and engineering. It has an excellent transportation system, boasting the TGV (*Train à Grande Vitesse*), below right. This is the world's fastest passenger train, with average speeds of over 130 mph. The electric car (below) is Renault's latest, energy-saving design. The rear wheels fold inward for easier parking.

Citroën

France is the world's fourth largest producer of cars. Only Japan, the United States and Germany make more. French cars, such as Citroën, Renault, and Peugeot, are world famous. The car-making factories are mainly found around Paris, Lyon, and Rennes. They use most of the metal produced by France's iron and steel industry. The medallions of the top three car manufacturers are shown

Renault

Peugeot

here. Renault is the largest of the three. France has a large network of roads. You have to pay a toll to drive on the highways, or *autoroutes.* Many people prefer the smaller *routes nationales,* or "N" roads.

The perfume industry
Some of the finest, most famous, and most expensive types of perfume are French. They include Chanel, Worth, and Dior. Perfume has been a major industry in France since the 1920s, although it has been made there since the sixteenth century. Flowers, such as lavender, are grown in the south. Their fragrance (called essential oil) is extracted to make delicate and costly scents. Grasse is where most French perfume is made.

Limoges porcelain

The town of Limoges, on the River Vienne, has been making fine porcelain since the eighteenth century. The industry had originally established itself in Sèvres during the 1750s, under the patronage of Louis XV. By the 1800s, however, Limoges had taken over as one of the largest porcelain centers in Europe. The Impressionist painter, Renoir (1841–1919), worked for a time as a porcelain painter in Limoges.

Those magnificent men

The French aircraft industry has been a pioneer in air travel. In 1793, the Montgolfier brothers made the first ever flight in a hot-air balloon. In 1874, Felix du Temple designed the first successful powered plane (pictured right). In 1903, the American Wright brothers made the first controlled and manned powered flight in their plane, *Flyer I.* This inspired the first flight in Europe, made in France by a Brazilian, Alberto Santos-Dumont in 1906. In 1909, Louis Blériot made the first flight across the English Channel. By the 1970s, France was manufacturing the Airbus A300 series (photo left).

Du Temple 1874

Santos-Dumont 14BIS 1906

Blériot XI 1909

Sabatier knives

Sabatier is a name chefs all over the world would recognize. For over one hundred years Sabatier has produced fine quality knives from French steel (see page 26). First established in 1885, Sabatier boast that their knives are forged from a single piece of steel. Next time you visit a kitchen store, look for the symbol of the lion, and the label, "Made in France."

The Concorde, the world's first supersonic passenger plane, first flew in 1969. It was a joint venture between the British and French. It has average cruising speed of over 1,240 mph.

The Concorde 1969

RESOURCES

To keep its industries running, France needs large amounts of raw materials. It has some natural resources (below) and it imports others, such as minerals and chemicals. Forests cover about one-quarter of France, making lumber a major natural resource. France does not have huge supplies of oil and gas. To supply energy to its factories, homes, and schools, it has turned to alternative forms of energy (bottom and below right), and invests huge amounts into the research of new energy sources such as nuclear power. Man-made resources include not only the tapping of these alternative supplies, but feats of building, such as the Channel Tunnel (below).

Mining resources
France has large supplies of coal, iron ore, and bauxite. It also has some oil, gas, and other minerals. These are mined and used in industry. Iron ore is particularly important for making steel for the car industry. The largest supplies of iron ore are found in the Lorraine area in the northeast. Bauxite (aluminum ore) is found in the southeast. It gets its name from the town of Les Baux. Aluminum is a light metal used to make drink cans and cooking foil.

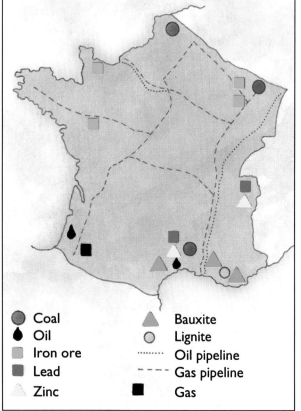

● Coal	▲ Bauxite
● Oil	○ Lignite
■ Iron ore	⋯⋯ Oil pipeline
■ Lead	‑‑‑ Gas pipeline
▲ Zinc	■ Gas

Tidal power
The world's first tidal power plant was built in 1966 at the mouth of the River Rance in Brittany. It extracts energy from the rise and fall of the tides. These tides can be extremely high, sometimes reaching a height of 43 feet. The energy in the water turns devices, called turbines, which are used to generate electricity. The French have also built a solar power plant at Odeillo in the Pyrénées. The sun's rays are concentrated using mirrors and are then used to heat water. The steam given off drives turbines. This is how the sun's energy is used to make electricity.

Marie Curie

Marie Curie (1867–1934) and her husband, Pierre Curie (1859–1906), are famous for their study of radioactivity and their discovery of the radioactive elements, radium and polonium. Marie also studied uranium, the main nuclear fuel. In 1903, they won the Nobel Prize for physics. In 1911, Marie won a second Nobel Prize, for chemistry, for her work in isolating radium. She also helped found the Radium Institute in Paris in 1914.

The Channel Tunnel is due to open in the mid-1990s. It consists of three tunnels – two rail tunnels and a service tunnel. Trains will carry passengers, cars, and goods under the sea between Folkestone, England, and Calais, France.

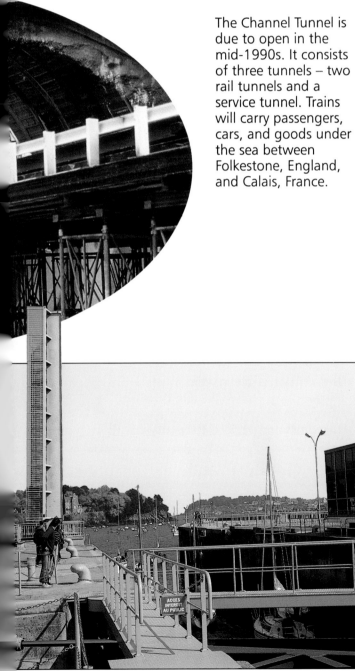

Nuclear power

Over one-third of France's electricity comes from nuclear energy and is produced in power plants like the one below. The rest comes from oil, gas, or coal, or from hydroelectric power plants, located in the Alps and Jura mountains. France is a world leader in nuclear research. Aiming for self-sufficiency, France produces its own nuclear fuels. It has one of the best safety records in the world. The French government considers it a clean and efficient source of energy and have invested huge sums in establishing new plants.

TODAY AND TOMORROW

France continues to have a great influence on the rest of the world through its art and culture, trade, language, scientific research, and its political ties. It is proud of its independent spirit, but also works closely with other countries in Europe and the rest of the world. France does suffer from some social problems, such as unemployment. But it also enjoys a high standard of living and is a world leader in agriculture and industry. Its mixture of traditional and modern culture has made it a very popular place to visit. The France of the future will continue to play a major part in world and European affairs, while remaining a proud and independent country.

France in space
The European Space Agency (ESA) has its headquarters in Paris. ESA was formed in 1975, and France is one of its most active members. It plans to launch a mini space shuttle, called *Hermès*, in 2003. *Hermès* was due to lift off on the back of the rocket, *Ariane 5*, and transport its ESA astronauts to the space station *Freedom*. The future of *Hermès*, however, looks doubtful, due to the possible withdrawal of Germany from the project.

Flag of United Nations

The Euro Parliament
Strasbourg, in northeast France, is the seat of the European Parliament. It meets to debate EC policies put forward by the Council of Ministers.

France and the UN
France is a leading member of the UN (United Nations). This international organization was set up after World War II to maintain peace and security and solve the social and economic problems faced by its members. Since France joined the UN in 1945, its troops have been part of peace-keeping forces around the world. Paris is the headquarters of UNESCO (the United Nations Educational, Scientific, and Cultural Organization).

Flag of the Council of Europe

The Council of Europe
The Council of Europe was established in 1949. Its headquarters are located in Strasbourg, France. Its aim is to promote economic and social progress among its 24 members.

The French foreign legion
The French foreign legion is an army of volunteers, mainly from countries outside France. It was formed by King Louis Philippe in 1831. Frenchmen are forbidden to join the Legion, but some enlist by giving false nationalities. Today it has about 8,000 members.

Médecins sans frontières

Médecins sans frontières (Doctors without frontiers) is a French charity that seeks to bring medical care to trouble-hit areas of the world. Its officials often risk their lives or risk being taken hostage to work in places such as the Middle East and Africa.

NATO

NATO

NATO (North Atlantic Treaty Organization) was established in 1950. France signed the North Atlantic Treaty in 1949 with 11 other nations. The treaty stated that an armed attack against one or more members in Europe or North America would be considered an attack against all members. Differences between France and the United States led to the withdrawal of French forces from NATO in 1966. NATO's headquarters are in Brussels, Belgium.

ESA

The European Space Agency promotes the development of a space program in Europe (see page 28). ESA supervised the building of *Spacelab* which was sent into orbit in 1983.

Tourism

France is one of the world's most popular tourist destinations. It has sandy beaches, mountains, forests, and picturesque towns and villages. The French Alps attract thousands of people every year to ski resorts such as Chamonix and Albertville. In April 1992, the EuroDisney resort opened in Marne-la-Vallée, about 18 miles outside Paris. One of its main attractions is Sleeping Beauty's castle (*Le château de la Belle au bois dormant*). The resort covers an area one-fifth the size of Paris, and employs thousands of people from all over the world.

AIDS research

France is at the forefront of present and future research into the disease AIDS. AIDS attacks the body's immune system and often results in death. The AIDS virus was identified in 1983 by a team of French researchers, led by Dr. Luc Montagnier of the Pasteur Institute in Paris. No cure for AIDS has been found, and research continues.

France is a country that embraces the future, while preserving the treasures of the past. French people now enjoy a standard of living that is higher than ever before, yet still strive to maintain their traditions and a culture that has succeeded in touching every corner of the world.

FACTS AND FIGURES

Name: La République Française (The French Republic)

Capital and largest city: Paris (population metropolitan area: 8.7 million)

National motto: Liberté, Egalité, Fraternité (Liberty, Equality, Fraternity)

Official language: French

Currency: French franc; 100 centimes make one franc

Population: 56,375,000

Population density: 252 people per sq mile

Life expectancy: 75 years

Distribution: 26% live in rural areas, 74% in towns and cities

Ethnic groups: About 93% French, about 7% recent immigrants – mostly from Indochina, Portugal, Spain, Turkey, Italy, Morocco, Tunisia, Algeria

Religion: 90% Roman Catholic, 3% Muslim, 2% Protestant, 2% Jewish

Area: 220,600 sq mi (551,500 sq km)

Size: Maximum east-west: 604 mi; north-south: 590 mi

Highest mountain: Mont Blanc 15,771 ft (4,807 m) in the Alps

Largest lake: Lac du Bourget, east of Lyon, 16.6 sq mi (43 sq km)

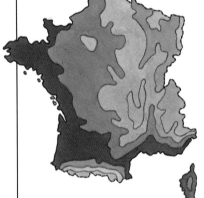

Degrees Fahrenheit/Celsius

	Above 40/Above 4
	36-40/2-4
	32-36/0 to 2
	Below 32/Below 0

AVERAGE JANUARY TEMPERATURES

Inches/Centimeters

	More than 40/More than 100
	32-40/80-100
	24-32/60-80
	Less than 24/Less than 60

AVERAGE ANNUAL RAINFALL

Degrees Fahrenheit/Celsius

	Above 72/Above 22
	68-72/20-22
	64-68/18-20
	Below 64/Below 18

AVERAGE JULY TEMPERATURES

Longest rivers: Loire, 628 mi (1,010 km); Rhône, 503 m (810 km); Seine, 478 mi (770 km); Garonne, 404 mi (650 km)

Climate: Summer – warm, winter – cool. On the Mediterranean coast, all the seasons are warmer (*See climate maps above*)

Location/physical features: On the western edge of Europe. Much of north-central, northern, and western France has either rolling hills or is flat.

Coastlines: on the Atlantic Ocean, Mediterranean Sea, and English Channel

Borders: with Belgium, Luxembourg, Germany, Switzerland, Italy, and Spain

Mountains: Pyrénées (forming the Spanish border), Alps (forming the Swiss and Italian borders), Juras (forming the Swiss border), Massif Central (in south-central France).

AGRICULTURE

Crop production (in millions of tons): wheat, 27; corn, 12; other cereals (including barley), 12; sugar beet, 25.7; (white sugar, 3.9); potatoes, 7.2; paper, 10.3; fruits, 1.6. Wine, 70.8 million hectoliters

Livestock: poultry, 218 million; cattle, 22.8 million; pigs, 12 million; sheep, 10.6 million; goats, 976,000; horses, 310,000

ECONOMY

One way to measure a country's wealth is to compare its Gross National Product (GNP) with those of other countries. The GNP is the total value of goods and services produced by a country in a year

Figures shown are 1990 GNPs in millions of US dollars

United States	5,465,000
USSR (former)	2,660,000
Japan	2,115,000
Germany	1,157,000
France	874,000
Great Britain	858,000
Italy	845,000

TOP 10 INDUSTRIAL IMPORTS

1. Cars
2. Crude petroleum
3. Computer equipment
4. Refined petroleum products
5. Car equipment
6. Organic chemicals
7. Planes
8. Plastics
9. Natural gas
10. Commercial vehicles

TOP 10 INDUSTRIAL EXPORTS

1. Cars
2. Car equipment
3. Planes
4. Organic chemicals
5. Computer equipment
6. Plastics
7. Iron and steel
8. Perfumes
9. Commercial vehicles
10. Pharmaceutical products

EXPORTS: (% sold to)

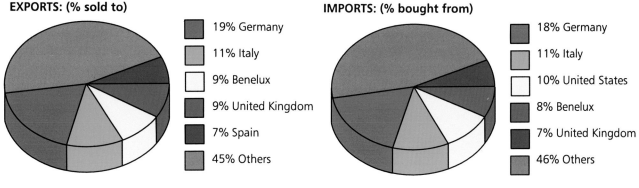

- 19% Germany
- 11% Italy
- 9% Benelux
- 9% United Kingdom
- 7% Spain
- 45% Others

IMPORTS: (% bought from)

- 18% Germany
- 11% Italy
- 10% United States
- 8% Benelux
- 7% United Kingdom
- 46% Others

INDUSTRY:

Main heavy industries: oil, 3.5 million tons; steel, 17.9 million tons; cement, 22.5 million tons; aluminum.

Also important: paper production, chemicals, textiles, food products, aircraft, motor manufacturing

ENERGY & MINERAL RESOURCES:

Oil and gas (1988): 3.5 million tons of crude oil; 10,000 m³ of natural gas. Most of the oil refined in France is imported.

Minerals: Mining represents less than 0.5% of GNP – coal, uranium, iron ore, sulfur, potash, copper, and bauxite

EUROPEAN COMMUNITY (EC) MEMBERS

1. France
2. Germany
3. United Kingdom
4. Ireland
5. Italy
6. Belgium
7. Luxembourg
8. Denmark
9. Greece
10. The Netherlands
11. Portugal
12. Spain

FAMOUS FACES

LITERATURE

Moliere (1622-1673) See page 4.

Racine, Jean (1639-99) One of the greatest French playwrights. Wrote during the French Classical Age. Almost all his plays are tragedies. Most famous works are *Phèdre* (1677) and *Andromache* (1667)

Hugo, Victor Marie (1802-1885) Poet, novelist, and dramatist who led the Romantic movement in French literature. Best known works are *The Hunchback of Notre Dame* (1831) and *Les Misérables* (1862).

Flaubert, Gustave (1821-1880) Flaubert's work is characterized by some of the most vivid and lifelike descriptions in literature. *Madame Bovary* (1856) is considered the most perfect french novel.

Verne, Jules (1828-1905) Wrote science fiction. Most famous works are *Twenty Thousand Leagues Under the Sea* (1870) and *Around The World in Eighty Days* (1873).

Zola, Emile (1840-1902) Began his career as a writer and novelist. His first novel of merit was *Thérèse Raquin* (1867) and his most famous work is *Germinal* (1885).

Proust, Marcel (1871-1922) Most famous works is *A la Recherche du Temps Perdu* (Remembrance of Things Past).

Sartre, Jean Paul (1905-1980) See page 15.

Beauvoir, Simone de (1908-1986) An author and philosopher whose ideas were similar to those of Sartre. Famous works include *The Second Sex* (1949) and *Memoirs of a Dutiful Daughter* (1958).

Cocteau, Jean (1889-1963) A controversial post, playwright, novelist, and artist. His best known novel is *Les Enfants Terribles*.

ART

Poussin, Nicholas (1594-1665) Believed painting should appeal to the mind, not the senses. Most of his subjects were taken from mythology or the Bible. Held the position of the First Painter to the King of France (Louis XIV).

Manet, Edouard (1832-1883) Often associated with the Impressionist style, Manet's work is renowned for its rich colors and textures. His most famous paintings include *Déjeuner Sur L'Herbe* (Luncheon on the Grass) and *Bar at the Folies Bergere*.

Cezanne, Paul(1839-1906) See page 11

Monet, Claude (1840-1926) A leader of the Impressionist movement. Especially concerned with the effect of outdoor light and atmosphere, he painted several series of pictures showing the effect of sunlight on a subject. This is shown in his series of paintings entitled *Water Lilies*.

Rodin, Auguste (1840-1917) One of the greatest sculptors of the 1800s, he was influenced by Michelangelo. One of his most important works is *The Gate of Hell*.

Renoir, Pierre Auguste (1841-1919) An Impressionist painter, famous for his pictures of young girls and children, and for his scenes of cheerful middle-class life.

Gaugin, Paul (1848-1903) Deliberately distorted nature by enclosing broad, flat areas of color with heavy contours. His pictures idealized the peoples of the South Sea islands.

Toulouse-Lautrec, Henri de (1864-1901) See page 15.

Matisse, Henri (1869-1954) One of the most influential artists of the 1900s. Leader of the Fauves, the first most important art movement of the era. Also a noted sculptor, book illustrator, and tapestry designer.

Degas, Edgar (1834-1917) A post-Impressionist painter and sculptor.

MUSIC

Bizet, Georges (1838-1875) Wrote *Carmen*, the most popular opera of all time. Was a brilliant pianist, although his main interest was in composing, especially operas.

Fauré, Gabriel Urbain (1845-1924) Composer of songs and song cycle (series of songs). Style characterized by an extensive use of harmony. Most famous works include *Requiem (1900), La Bonne Chanson (1894)* and *La Chanson d'Eve (1906-10)*.

Debussy, Claude (1862-1918) Greatly influenced by language and literature in his work. Was the leader of impressionism in music, and his radical style helped to change the direction of music in the early 1900s. Most famous work is *Clair de Lune* (Moonlight)

Ravel, Maurice(1875-1937) Work reflects Spanish influence in life. Most popular composition is the ballet music, *Bolero* (1928).

SCIENCE

Descartes, René (1596-1650) A scientist, philosopher, and mathematician. He invented analytic geometry and was a pioneer in the attempt to develop universal laws of motion.

Pascal, Blaise (1623-1662) A physicist, mathematician, and philosopher. His work on the pressure of fluids produced the principle, Pascal's law.

Lavoisier, Antoine Laurent (1743-1794) The founder of modern chemistry. He studied combustion and discovered and named oxygen. Lavoisier published his findings in his *Elementary Treatise on Chemistry* (1798).

Cuvier, Baron (1769-1832) A naturalist who pioneered the founding of paleontology (the study of fossils). He wrote a book on zoology, *The Animal Kingdom*.

Daguerre, Louis Jacques Mandé (1787-1851) Introduced the first popular form of photography. His pictures were called daguerreotypes.

Braille, Louis (1809-1852) See page 2.

Pasteur, Louis (1822-1895) See page 23.

Curie, Marie (1867-1934) See page 2.

Bleriot, Louis (1872-1936) See page 25.

Cousteau, Jacques-Yves (1910-) An oceanographer, author, and film producer. In 1943, he invented the aqualung. He explored the oceans in his research ship Calypso and promoted their conservation.

ENCORE!...

Clovis I (466?-511) A Frankish king who defeated the last great Roman army in Gaul (now called France).

Joan of Arc (1412?-1431) See pages 6/7.

Louis XIV (1638-1715) See page 7.

Marie Antoinette (1755-1793) Became queen of France after marrying Louis XVI, and died on the guillotine during the French Revolution. She became unpopular with the people due to her frivolities. Is best known for her phrase, *Then let them eat cake*, in response to the Parisians' anger at having no bread.

Robespierre (1758-1794) The most famous and controversial leader of the French Revolution (see page 8). He helped bring about the Reign of Terror in which thousands of people were executed.

Napoleon I (1769-1821) See page 8.

De Gaulle, Charles (1890-1970) Became the outstanding French soldier and statesman of the 1900s. He led the French resistance in World War II and formed the Fifth Republic in 1958. He was president for 11 years.

Mitterrand, Francois-Maurice (1916-) Elected president of France in 1981 and again in 1988. He was the first socialist president since 1958.

FRENCH WORDS USED IN ENGLISH

adieu goodbye
à la mode fashionable
à propos by the way
au fait to the point; familiar with
avant-garde ahead of the times
beau monde fashionable society
bête noire a person or thing that is especially disliked
carte blanche to be given absolute power or authority
cause célèbre a cause that arouses public feeling
c'est la vie that's life
comme il faut as it should be
coup de grâce the final blow
crème de la crème the best
cri de coeur heartfelt cry or appeal
crime passionel a crime provoked by passion
de rigeur necessary according to custom
déjà vu a sense of having seen before
éminence grise a person who wields power behind the scenes
entente cordiale an informal, friendly understanding between nations
en masse in a large body
entre nous between ourselves
esprit de corps group spirit
fait accompli an irreversible fact
faux pas a bad mistake
haute couture high fashion
idée fixe an obsession
je ne sais quois a distinct quality that cannot be described
jeu d'esprit witty comment
joie de vivre love of life
laissez-faire to leave alone
mot juste the exact expresssion
noblesse oblige obligations imposed because of rank
nouveau riche ostentatious from newly-acquired wealth
par excellence to the highest degree
passé old fashioned
pièce de résistance something outstanding
raison d'être reason for being
risqué indelicate or suggestive
sang-froid calm self-control in the face of difficulty
savoir-faire to know how to act appropriately
soi-disant so called
tête-à-tête a head to head, intimate conversation
tour de force an outstanding feat
vis-à-vis relative to, compared with
voilà there you have it
volte-face to do an about-face

INDEX

Photographic Credits:
Abbreviations: T (top), M (middle), L (left), B (bottom), R (right) Front cover T: Planet Earth Pics; Front cover M & 7T, 13BL, 15TL & 28-29: Eye Ubiquitous; front cover BL, 2, 5B, 7B, 8, 12-13, 13BR, 14T&M, 15TR, 16-17 all, 18BR, 20T, 22T, ML & B2, 24T, 25T, 26T, 28T, & 29BR: Charles de Vere; front BR, back TR, title p, 18BL, 23, 24BL & 25B: Roger Vlitos; back TL, 5T, 11B, 12T, BL & R, 15B, 18T, 24BR & 27L: Spectrum Colour Library; back M: Bruce Coleman Ltd; 6, 9B, 14B, 19T & B, 20 L & R, 21T L& B, 24MR, 26M, 27R, 28M, 29T, M&BL: Frank Spooner; 9T: Hulton Deutsch; 9M, 13T, 21TR & 28B: Mary Evans PL; 10 & 22MR: Angela Graham; 11L & R: Courtauld Inst. Galleries;18M: Robert harding